THE WORLD'S 60 BEST RECIPES FOR STUDENTS... PERIOD.
VÉRONIQUE PARADIS

PHOTOGRAPHER: Antoine Sicotte
ART DIRECTOR: Antoine Sicotte
GRAPHIC DESIGNER: Laurie Auger
COVER DESIGNER: Laurie Auger
FOOD STYLIST: Véronique Paradis
ENGLISH TRANSLATOR: Lorien Jones
COPY EDITOR: Anna Phelan

PROJECT EDITOR: Antoine Ross Trempe

ISBN: 978-2-920943-44-5

©2012, CARDINAL PUBLISHERS / LES ÉDITIONS CARDINAL
All rights reserved.

Legal Deposit: 2012
Bibliothèque et Archives du Québec
Library and Archives Canada
ISBN: 978-2-920943-44-5

The publisher acknowledges the financial support of the Government of Canada through the Canada Book Fund (CBF) for its publishing activities and the support of the Government of Quebec through the tax credits for book publishing program (SODEC).

Originally published under the title *"Les 60 meilleures recettes pour étudiants du monde... Point final."*

PRINTED IN CANADA

RECIPES FOR STUDENTS

PERIOD.

THE WORLD'S 60 BEST

RECIPES FOR STUDENTS

PERIOD.

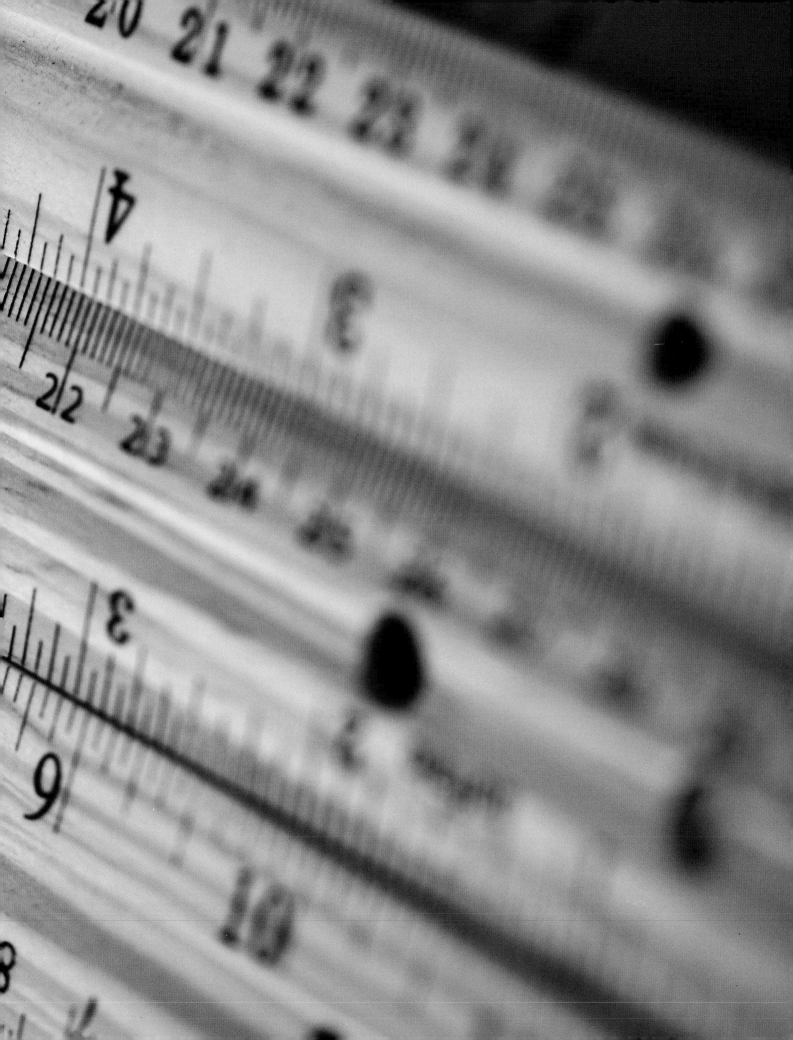

ABOUT THIS BOOK

The 60 recipes in this book are, in our opinion, the 60 best recipes for students in the world. Our team of chefs, writers and gourmets explored everything the culinary world has to offer to create this collection of the world's 60 best recipes for students.

We based our recipes on the following criteria:

QUALITY OF INGREDIENTS
ORIGINALITY
TASTE
APPEARANCE
SIMPLICITY

Are these our personal favorite student recipes? Of course! But rest assured, our team of passionate, dedicated gourmets put time and loving care into formulating and testing each recipe in order to provide you with the 60 best recipes ever. In fact, our chef brought each freshly made dish straight from the kitchen into the studio—no colorants, no sprays, no special effects added—and after each photo shoot, our creative team happily devoured the very dishes you see in these photos.

We hope you'll enjoy discovering these recipes and using this book as much as we enjoyed making it.

TABLE OF CONTENTS

INTRO

Every one of the 60 best recipes in this book features a flavor and cost legend (see pages 018 and 019) to guide your taste buds as well as your wallet in choosing the perfect dish. You will also find a glossary of culinary terms (page 029), handy cooking tips and tricks (page 025), and a list of must-have kitchen tools (page 023) that will help you create the world's BEST recipes. Finally, use the easy-to-follow Table of Contents (pages 010 and 011) and Ingredients Index (pages 176 to 181) to find everything you're looking for.

Impress guests with your food knowledge from our informative "Did You Know?" sidebars, and take your meals to the next level thanks to our chef's tips, supersaver's tips, and gourmet variations!

Bon appétit!

TIME DIFFICULTY SPICY RICH COST

LEGEND

 PREPARATION TIME IN MINUTES, INCLUDING COOKING TIME

LEVEL OF DIFFICULTY

 BEGINNER   INTERMEDIATE   EXPERT

HOT • PEPPERY • ZESTY

 LOW    MEDIUM   HIGH

CREAMY • BUTTERY • LUSCIOUS

 LOW   MEDIUM   HIGH

COST OF INGREDIENTS

 LOW   MEDIUM   HIGH

A SHORT HISTORY OF STUDENT MEALS

Times are changing! Back in the day, our grandmothers and great-grandmothers were taught at an early age how to cook, clean, and take care of a family. But our parents didn't always have the time to teach us basic cooking skills, and didn't have access to the wide array of foods that we're lucky to have today.

Today, many young people start college with zero culinary knowledge, few kitchen tools, and little money to spend on food. They often lack smart grocery shopping skills and have to learn not only how to budget, but also to: plan meals in advance to avoid impulse purchases; make healthy choices; and avoid wasting food. Being a student isn't easy: students are busy, tired, and cash-strapped, and after juggling classes, homework, part-time jobs, and sports, they just don't feel like cooking for themselves. More often than not, students resort to prepackaged, ready-made meals or grab a meal at a fast food chain, which is usually the most affordable restaurant option, but almost always higher in salt and fat.

And yet, students are constantly bombarded with ads, commercials, and news stories about the importance of a healthy diet. Maintaining a healthy lifestyle is especially important when there's an exam to study for or a sports competition coming up, or just to stay alert during the long periods of concentration required on any regular school day. So how do we break the cycle of poor diet? With information about proper nutrition at our fingertips and the wide variety of products available to us, we can easily debunk the myth of the student diet and prove that yes, you can cook healthy, affordable meals with just a few basic kitchen staples. And yes, you can eat in front of the computer, or even in bed!

We've created *The World's 60 Best Recipes for Students* to help busy students save time and money and develop better eating habits. It's truly an all-in-one guide!

MUST-HAVE TOOLS

WHAT YOU NEED TO MAKE THE WORLD'S BEST RECIPES

1. **Aluminum foil** for cooking *en papillote* (in a parcel), for preventing food from sticking to baking pans, and for covering frying pans or pots

2. A **casserole dish** for gratins, casseroles, and roasts

3. A **large pot** for pasta and for cooking large quantities

4. A **large frying pan** for frying and sautéing

5. A **small pot** for making sauces and for cooking individual portions

6. A **potato masher** for making delicious mashed potatoes

7. A **rectangular baking sheet** for pizzas, quesadillas, chicken wings, and more

8. A **grater** for grating cheese and vegetables

9. A **colander** for draining and straining

10. A **can opener** for opening cans of all sizes

11. A **spatula** for flipping food without breaking it

12. A **good quality knife** for chopping, cubing, dicing, and mincing

13. A **wooden spoon** for mixing, tossing, and stirring

14. A **cutting board** for chopping and for keeping your cooking area clean

15. A **large bowl** for mixing salads and more

16. A **pair of tongs** for flipping grilled meats and vegetables

17. A **vegetable peeler** for peeling all kinds of vegetables and fruit

18. A **whisk** for preparing crêpes, mayonnaise, vinaigrettes, and more

19. A **measuring cup** for measuring out exact quantities for perfect results every time

20. A **hand blender**, which is a great investment for any student—it reduces clean up and makes many cooking tasks quicker and easier, like puréeing soups right in the pot, or making pestos, dips, milkshakes, and more

TIPS & TRICKS

FOR CREATING THE WORLD'S BEST STUDENT RECIPES

1. Keep your work area clean and organized. Get a cutting board for easy clean up, wash your hands thoroughly, and you'll be good to go! Having a workspace you enjoy will encourage you to cook at home, helping you to learn and grow in the kitchen.

2. Fresh food from nature that hasn't been processed, packaged or refined is often more affordable. Opt for meat that hasn't been pre-marinated, fresh whole vegetables, and cheese and lunchmeat that has been sliced and cut at the grocery store. Plan your meals around the weekly specials on fresh food that your local supermarket has to offer and you may be surprised at how much you'll save!

3. Some recipes might use a food or a brand that you're unfamiliar with or unsure where to get. Do a quick Internet search to find out what it is and where to buy it—you might just discover your new favorite ingredient!

4. It's important to have at least one good knife, but chef's knives are almost always expensive. Luckily, affordable, good quality knives can usually be found at Asian grocery stores, and even the dollar store.

5. Don't spend a fortune on new supplies for your kitchen—gently used equipment and utensils work just as well. Search bazaars, garage sales, and your grandparents' cupboards for the items you need, but remember that the more you have, the more you'll need to wash!

6. Organize potlucks or group cooking sessions. Get together with a few friends to swap ideas, recipes, and even kitchen equipment. There's no better combination than learning while having fun!

7. Make sure to read through and understand the recipe before you start cooking. Gather all of the necessary ingredients and equipment beforehand and preheat the oven if you need to. Preparation is key!

8. The more you experiment in the kitchen, the more you'll learn. Try different techniques and don't hesitate to add or substitute ingredients. Cook with what you've got on hand, and above all, cook what you like.

9. Keep this book in the kitchen and use it as a shopping guide. Keep track of the approximate cost of each recipe you've tried, any substitutions you've made, and which recipes you use for school lunches, dinners, and entertaining. Think of this book as another piece of kitchen equipment—don't be afraid to get it a little dirty during cooking!

10. Finally, remember that the best recipes are always made using the freshest ingredients. Eat fresh!

HOW-TO GUIDE

Now it's time to stock your shelves and fill your refrigerator. But where to start? What items should you always have on hand and how do you avoid spending a fortune at the grocery store? Here's a starter's guide to nutritious, affordable food basics that won't break the bank and will help you create recipes to fuel your study sessions. Consult this shopping list before heading out grocery shopping, and add fresh food like fruits and vegetables, meat, and dairy depending on what's in season and on special, your budget for the week, and the recipes you want to try.

GROCERY STAPLES

SPICES
- Cinnamon
- Chili powder
- Curry powder
- Crushed red pepper flakes
- Italian seasoning
- Steak spice
- Cumin
- Salt
- Pepper

DRY GOODS
- Couscous
- White flour
- Baking powder
- White sugar
- Breadcrumbs
- White rice
- Olive oil
- Vegetable oil
- Short pasta
- Spaghetti

CANNED GOODS
- Chicken stock or chicken bouillon cubes
- Diced tomatoes
- Tomato paste
- Crushed tomatoes
- Tomato juice
- Tuna
- Gravy
- Chickpeas
- Mixed beans

CONDIMENTS
- Soy sauce
- Peanut butter
- Mayonnaise
- Honey
- Ketchup
- Dijon mustard
- Balsamic vinegar
- White vinegar
- Hot sauce of your choice: Tabasco, sambal oelek, sriracha, piri-piri, harissa, etc.

FOR A LITTLE SOMETHING EXTRA: fresh Parmesan cheese, butter, Arborio rice, fresh garlic, coconut milk, onions, basil pesto, pickles, vanilla extract, tahini

GLOSSARY

1. SEASON

To improve the flavor of a dish by adding salt and pepper to taste.

2. BLANCH

To cook vegetables briefly in boiling, salted water.

3. EMULSION

A mixture of two or more liquids or substances that normally can't be combined. An emulsifier such as egg yolk or mustard is often added to prevent separation.

4. DICE

A basic knife cut in which food is cut into cubes.

5. DEGLAZE

To remove and dissolve caramelized bits of food at the bottom of a pan in order to make a jus or a sauce.

6. THINLY SLICE

To cut into thin, equal slices.

7. SAUTÉ

To cook, stirring, over high heat in a pan, Dutch oven, or heavy-bottomed pot.

8. CHOP

To cut into small pieces with a sharp instrument (knife or food processor).

9. REDUCE

To thicken a liquid by evaporation over heat.

10. JULIENNE

A basic knife cut in which food is cut into long, thin strips. A mandoline is often used for this cut.

11. SEAR

To cook in fat (butter or oil) at a high temperature to obtain a golden or brown crust.

12. ZEST

To remove the zest (outer skin) of citrus fruits with a zester, grater, or peeling knife.

THE CHEF'S SECRET

Every seasoned chef will attest that the real secret to creating a successful dish is to *taste! taste! taste!* Taste before and after seasoning, add some heat or a squeeze of lemon juice if you think your dish needs a little kick, or go ahead and double the herbs or even the cheese! The most important thing is to follow your instincts and your senses. Listen for that telltale sizzle, inhale the tantalizing aromas, and CONSTANTLY taste your food so you can get to know your dish in all its stages.

There you have it—the simple secret to creating delicious, original dishes.

GUACAMOLE & SALSA DUO

SERVES 4

FOR GUACAMOLE

1 avocado, pit removed and flesh scooped out
Juice of 1 lime
2 tbsp olive oil
Salt and pepper

FOR SALSA

1 shallot, chopped
1 can (14 oz) diced tomatoes, drained
1 jalapeño pepper, seeded and finely chopped
1/2 tsp cumin
2 tbsp olive oil
1/4 cup (60 ml) fresh cilantro, chopped (optional)
Salt and pepper
Hot sauce to taste

PREPARATION

For guacamole: In a bowl, mash avocado and lime juice with a fork. Add olive oil and season with salt and pepper. Mix well, about 1 minute. Serve.

For salsa: In a bowl, combine all ingredients. Serve.

 **DID YOU KNOW?**

In Spanish, the word *salsa* refers to any type of sauce, but the term also designates a popular dance and musical style.

FRIES & MAYO

SERVES 4

FOR FRIES

4 large potatoes, cut into wedges
2 tbsp olive oil or vegetable oil
1 tsp chili powder
Salt and pepper

FOR HOMEMADE MAYONNAISE

1 egg yolk
1 tbsp Dijon mustard
Juice of 1/2 lemon
1/2 cup (125 ml) vegetable oil
Salt and pepper

PREPARATION

For fries: In a bowl, combine all ingredients. Spread fries in a single layer on a baking sheet. Cook in a 400°F (200°C) oven for 40 minutes or until potatoes are golden brown and fully cooked through.

For homemade mayonnaise: In a large bowl, combine egg, Dijon mustard, and lemon juice. Whisk vigorously for 2 minutes. Add oil in a slow, steady stream, whisking constantly until mayonnaise is creamy. Season with salt and pepper.

If mayonnaise is too thick or too oily, add a few drops of warm water to thin it out.

DID YOU KNOW?

Homemade mayonnaise will keep in the refrigerator for 2 to 3 weeks.

CHOCOLATE FONDUE

SERVES 2

INGREDIENTS

1/2 cup (125 ml) dark chocolate (70% cocoa), in pieces
1 cup (250 ml) 35% cream

2 cups (500 ml) fruit of your choice
(bananas, apples, pears, grapes, strawberries, etc.)

PREPARATION

In a small microwave-safe bowl, combine chocolate and cream. Microwave for 1 minute. Stir with a fork. Cook for another 45 seconds and then stir until mixture is smooth. Serve with fresh fruit.

GOURMET VARIATION

A splash of kirsch or rum is often added to chocolate fondue, much like in traditional Swiss fondue recipes.

MASHED POTATOES 5 WAYS

SERVES 2

DID YOU KNOW?

Store tofu in water and it will keep for 7 to 10 days in the refrigerator, so long as the water is changed every day.

THE BASICS

3 yellow-fleshed potatoes, peeled and quartered

CLASSIC MASHED POTATOES

2 tbsp butter
1/4 cup (60 ml) milk
Salt and pepper

LIGHTEN UP! MASHED POTATOES

1/2 cup (125 ml) chicken or vegetable stock
Salt and pepper

CREAMY MASHED POTATOES

1/2 cup (125 ml) sour cream
Salt and pepper

HIPPIE MASHED POTATOES

1/2 cup (125 ml) soft tofu
Salt and pepper

DELUXE MASHED POTATOES

1/2 cup (125 ml) old cheddar, grated
1/4 cup (60 ml) chives, chopped
2 tbsp butter
1/4 cup (60 ml) milk
Salt and pepper

PREPARATION

Place potatoes in a pot and cover with water. Add 1 tsp salt and bring to a boil. Let simmer for 15 minutes. Drain.

Mash with a potato masher or a fork (potato masher is recommended).

Add desired ingredients and mix. Don't over-mix, as the potatoes will become gluey.

5

DULCE
DE LECHE

10 OZ

 **DID YOU KNOW?**

In Spanish, *dulce de leche* means "candy milk," This sweet, gooey treat is believed to have originated in Argentina, where it is often used as a spread, as a filling for cookies and chocolates, in cakes, and much, much more.

INGREDIENTS

1 can (10 oz) sweetened condensed milk

PREPARATION

Do not open can, but remove paper.

Place can in a pot and cover with water. Cover and let simmer for 1 hour 30 minutes.

Let can cool until warm, open, and serve over ice cream, apple pie, or any of your favorite desserts.

EASY ZUCCHINI

SERVES 1

 SUPERSAVER'S TIP

When the weather starts heating up, buy a fresh mint plant—it thrives as a houseplant, doesn't cost much money, and will brighten up your kitchen! And of course, you'll have fresh, fragrant mint on hand for tea and fresh fruit salads.

INGREDIENTS

1 tbsp olive oil
1 zucchini, cut into 1/2-inch rounds
1 clove garlic, chopped
Juice of 1/2 lemon
Salt
4 leaves fresh mint, chopped

PREPARATION

Heat oil in a pan. Add zucchini and let cook, undisturbed, until golden brown, about 2 minutes. Add garlic, lemon juice, and salt. Stir and continue cooking for 1 minute. Stir in mint and serve.

EXPRESS BOLOGNESE

SERVES 6

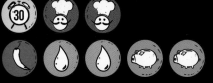

GOURMET VARIATION

For vegetarian sauce, substitute 2 cups (500 ml) drained and rinsed brown lentils for the ground beef.

CHEF'S TIP

Pasta is truly a student's best friend. Cook up a big batch of this versatile sauce—it only takes 30 minutes—divide it into individual portions, and freeze. Just pop a single serving in the microwave for a no-fuss meal!

SUPERSAVER'S TIP

Try this sauce with ground pork—it's less expensive than ground beef and just as delicious!

INGREDIENTS

1 tbsp vegetable oil
1 onion, diced
1 lb ground beef
1 can (6 oz) tomato paste
1 can (14 oz) tomato juice
1 can (28 oz) crushed tomatoes
1 tbsp sugar
1 tbsp Italian seasoning
Salt and pepper

PREPARATION

In a pot, heat oil and sauté onion. Add ground beef. When meat is completely cooked, add remaining ingredients. Let simmer for 15 minutes, stirring occasionally. Serve over pasta of your choice.

FUNKY FISH RAGOUT

SERVES 2

INGREDIENTS

1 tbsp olive oil or vegetable oil
1 leek, thinly sliced
1 clove garlic, chopped
1/2 cup (125 ml) white rice
1 cup (250 ml) tomato juice
1 cup (250 ml) water
1 fillet (about 1/2 lb) white fish (halibut, flounder, haddock, etc.), cut into 1-inch cubes
Salt and pepper
1/4 cup (60 ml) fresh cilantro, roughly chopped

PREPARATION

In a pot, heat oil and sauté leek and garlic for 2 minutes. Add rice and cook, stirring, for 1 minute, and then add tomato juice and water. Let simmer over low heat for 10 minutes. Add fish, season with salt and pepper, and continue cooking for 2 minutes. Remove from heat, cover, and let sit for 5 minutes. Stir in cilantro and serve.

GOURMET VARIATION

If you like your food spicy, add your favorite hot sauce to this dish, which is inspired by Portuguese cuisine.

DID YOU KNOW?

White fish is low in fat and a good source of protein but, unlike salmon and other fatty fish, isn't rich in Omega-3 fatty acids.

MINTY ONE-POT MEATBALLS

SERVES 2

FOR KOFTA

1/2 lb ground pork
6 leaves fresh mint, chopped
1 tbsp Ras el hanout (Moroccan spice blend)
1 onion, finely chopped
Salt

INGREDIENTS

1 tbsp olive oil or vegetable oil
2 cups (500 ml) store-bought tomato sauce
1 tbsp hot sauce (or to taste)
1/2 cup (125 ml) water
1/2 cup (125 ml) couscous

PREPARATION

In a bowl, combine kofta ingredients. Form 6 small patties.

In a large pan, heat oil over medium heat and cook koftas for 3 to 4 minutes on each side. Pour tomato sauce and water into pan and continue cooking for 3 minutes. Add hot sauce. Add couscous to sauce, trying not to pour any couscous onto patties. Cook for 1 minute. Cover and remove from heat. Let sit for 5 minutes. Serve.

 SUPERSAVER'S TIP

Ground pork is inexpensive, but you can also use ground beef or even lamb.

10

TUNA AVOCADO BOATS

SERVES 2

 **CHEF'S TIP**

Here's what to look for when buying an avocado:

A ready-to-eat avocado is dark, almost black in color.

Don't buy a mushy avocado—it will have blackened flesh that is unusable.

If the avocado is green, it isn't ripe yet.

A ripe avocado should yield to gentle pressure and the flesh should be green and easily scooped out with a spoon.

If you prefer, buy a green avocado and store it at room temperature. It will ripen in two or three days.

INGREDIENTS

1 avocado
1 can (6 oz) flaked tuna, drained
2 tbsp mayonnaise
1 tsp hot sauce
Salt and pepper

PREPARATION

With a small knife, cut avocado lengthwise around the pit. Twist the two halves to open. With a spoon, remove pit.

In a bowl, combine tuna, mayonnaise, hot sauce, salt, and pepper.

Serve tuna salad in avocado halves.

11

BREAKFAST MILKSHAKE

SERVES 1

INGREDIENTS

1-1/2 cups (375 ml) milk
1 banana
1 tbsp peanut butter
1 tbsp wheat germ (optional)

PREPARATION

With a hand blender, purée all ingredients.
Drink before heading to class!

12

FISH & CHIPS

SERVES 4

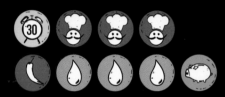

FOR FISH

Vegetable oil for frying

1/2 bottle (6 oz) dark beer
1/2 cup (125 ml) flour + 1 tbsp flour to coat fish
Salt and pepper

1 lb white fish (cod, tilapia, haddock, sole, etc.),
cut into 2-inch x 5-inch diagonal strips

FOR TARTAR SAUCE

1/4 cup (60 ml) mayonnaise
2 tbsp pickles of your choice, finely chopped
or sweet relish

Lemon wedges for garnish

PREPARATION

In a small bowl, combine tartar sauce ingredients. Refrigerate.

In a bowl, whisk together beer, 1/2 cup (125 ml) flour, salt, and pepper. Refrigerate for 15 minutes.

Pour 2 inches of oil into a large pot. Heat oil. Oil is ready for cooking when small drops of batter sprinkled onto the surface start to sizzle.

When oil is ready, coat fish in a bit of flour and dip in batter. Carefully place battered fish in oil and fry until crisp and golden. Remove with a slotted spoon or tongs and drain on a paper towel.

Serve with tartar sauce, lemon wedges, and fries (see recipe on page 034).

DID YOU KNOW?

In England, fish and chips was traditionally served in newspaper. These days, it is usually served in food-quality wrapping paper.

13

STUFFED TOMATOES

SERVES 4

INGREDIENTS

2 Italian sausages, hot or mild
2 slices bread, cut into small cubes
1 tbsp balsamic vinegar
4 medium tomatoes
2 tbsp Parmesan cheese

PREPARATION

With a small knife, make a cut down the side of each sausage and push out meat. Put sausage meat, cubed bread, and vinegar into a large bowl. With your hands, knead until mixture is well blended.

Cut off tomato tops and, using a spoon, carefully scoop out the inner flesh and seeds. Stuff tomatoes with sausage mixture and sprinkle with Parmesan cheese. Place on a baking sheet and cook in a 350°F (175°C) oven for 20 minutes. Serve.

 SUPERSAVER'S TIP

This recipe is perfect for a dinner party on a budget. Make extras and reheat the next day for lunch!

14

THE PHILLY STEAK

SERVES 1

INGREDIENTS

1 tbsp olive oil or vegetable oil
1/2 onion, thinly sliced
1/2 red pepper, cut into strips
4 slices roast beef, cut into thin strips
1 can (14 oz) gravy
1/2 baguette
1 slice provolone or Swiss cheese, cut in half (optional)

PREPARATION

Put gravy in a bowl and microwave for 2 minutes.

In a large pan, heat oil and sauté onion and pepper until soft. Add roast beef and 1/2 cup (125 ml) gravy. Reduce until sauce is thick and coats beef.

Cut baguette and top first with cheese, then meat and vegetable mixture. Close sandwich. Serve with remaining gravy on the side for dipping.

DID YOU KNOW?

The famous Philly cheese steak made its official debut in 1930 when two brothers began selling chopped steak on hoagie rolls at their Philadelphia hot dog stand. Since then, the sandwich has become a regional specialty and a cultural obsession.

15

MEXI RICE

SERVES 4

INGREDIENTS

1 tbsp olive oil
1 onion, thinly sliced
1/2 lb ground beef
1 cup (250 ml) white rice
1 tsp cumin
1 cup (250 ml) tomato juice
1 cup (250 ml) water
2 fresh tomatoes, diced
10 leaves fresh mint, chopped
Hot sauce to taste
Salt and pepper

PREPARATION

In a pan, heat oil and sauté onion and ground beef. When meat is cooked, add rice and cumin. Cook for 1 minute and then add tomato juice, water, and diced tomatoes. Let simmer for 10 minutes, or until rice is cooked. If rice is still crunchy, add a bit of water, and continue cooking until tender. Stir in mint and hot sauce, season with salt and pepper, and serve.

GOURMET VARIATION

Add peppers, zucchini, eggplant, or any other vegetables of your choice to boost flavor and nutritional value.

HEARTY HOMEMADE SOUP

SERVES 6

INGREDIENTS

1 tbsp olive oil or vegetable oil
1 onion, diced
2 carrots, peeled and cut into 1/4-inch rounds
2 cloves garlic, chopped
6 new potatoes, quartered
1 can (28 oz) diced tomatoes
4 cups water, or chicken or vegetable stock
1 tbsp Italian seasoning
Salt and pepper
10 green beans, cut into 1-inch pieces
2 zucchinis, cut into cubes
1/2 cup (125 ml) soup noodles

PREPARATION

In a large pot, heat oil and sauté onion and carrots for 2 minutes. Add garlic and potatoes and cook for another 2 minutes. Add tomatoes, water or stock, and Italian seasoning. Season with salt and pepper and let simmer for 15 minutes.

Add green beans, zucchini, and soup noodles. Cook for 5 minutes, remove from heat, and serve.

 **CHEF'S TIP**

Save and freeze your leftover Parmesan rinds—they add a wonderfully rich, buttery flavor to homemade soups! Just toss the rinds in along with the onion and remove right before serving.

TUNA PASTA

SERVES 4

INGREDIENTS

2 cups (500 ml) short pasta
2 tbsp olive oil
2 fresh tomatoes, diced
1 can (6 oz) flaked tuna, drained
1/4 cup (60 ml) store-bought basil or sundried tomato pesto
Salt and pepper

PREPARATION

Bring a large pot of water to a boil. Add pasta and cook according to package directions. Drain and set aside.

In the same pot, heat oil and add tomatoes and tuna. Cook for 1 minute. Add pesto and pasta and season with salt and pepper. Mix well and serve.

DID YOU KNOW?

Fresh and canned tuna both contain Omega-3 fatty acids, which are necessary for human health but which the body doesn't produce on its own.

OCEAN DELIGHT

SERVES 2

INGREDIENTS

1 bag (about 2 lbs) mussels
1 tbsp olive oil or vegetable oil
3 cloves garlic, chopped
1/2 cup (125 ml) olives, chopped
4 green onions, thinly sliced
1 can (28 oz) diced tomatoes

PREPARATION

Rinse mussels under cold water. Discard any broken or open mussels.

In a large pot, heat oil and cook garlic, olives, and green onions for 2 minutes. Add tomatoes and mussels. Stir and cover. Cook until mussels open.

Shaking the pot occasionally will help shells open up.

Serve with French fries and mayonnaise, or over pasta.

DID YOU KNOW?

Mussels are still alive when you buy them. Storing mussels in an airtight container will kill them, so keep them in the refrigerator covered with a damp dish towel instead. Check any open shells by tapping them. If the shell closes right away, the mussel is alive. If it stays open, the mussel is dead and should be discarded.

CHOW MEIN

SERVES 4

FOR MARINADE

3 tbsp soy sauce
1 tbsp peanut butter
1 tbsp ketchup
1/2 tsp chili powder

FOR CHOW MEIN

1/2 block firm tofu (about 1/2 lb), cut into 1-inch cubes

1 tbsp olive oil or vegetable oil
1 yellow pepper, cut into thin strips
1 cup (250 ml) snow peas, halved
2 cups (500 ml) bean sprouts
1/4 cup (60 ml) fresh cilantro, chopped

PREPARATION

In a large bowl, combine marinade ingredients. Add tofu and gently toss to coat. Refrigerate for at least 2 hours (maximum 2 days).

In a large pan, heat oil and cook yellow pepper strips. Add tofu, remaining marinade, and snow peas. Cook for 5 minutes. Stir in bean sprouts and fresh cilantro. Serve.

20

DIVINE CAULIFLOWER

SERVES 4

INGREDIENTS

1 cauliflower
1 tbsp curry powder
1/3 cup (80 ml) olive oil
2 tbsp honey or real maple syrup
Salt and pepper

PREPARATION

Cut cauliflower into medium florets.

In a bowl, combine curry powder, oil, and honey or real maple syrup. Add cauliflower and toss to coat. Season with salt and pepper. Spread cauliflower in a single layer on a baking sheet and broil in the oven or grill on the barbecue for 10 minutes. Serve.

GOURMET VARIATION

This makes a great side dish for grilled meat or fish!

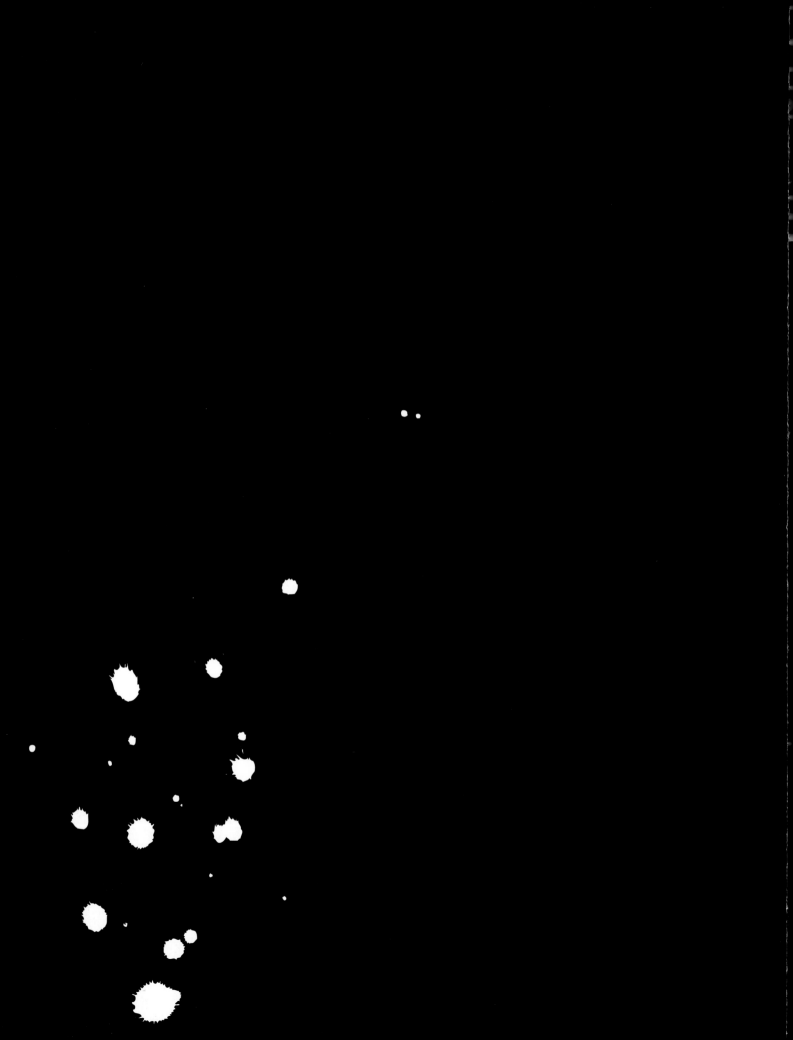

21

HUEVOS RANCHEROS

SERVES 2

INGREDIENTS

1 cup (250 ml) store-bought or homemade salsa
(see recipe on page 032)
1 cup (250 ml) canned black beans, drained and rinsed
4 eggs
1/2 cup (125 ml) Monterey jack cheese, grated
Salt and pepper

PREPARATION

In a pan, gently cook salsa and black beans. Make 4 small hollows in salsa and bean mixture and break one egg into each. Season with salt and pepper. Add grated cheese, cover, and cook for 2 minutes.

Serve with toast or tortillas.

 **DID YOU KNOW?**

Huevos rancheros is a popular Mexican breakfast dish that was traditionally served to farm workers as a mid-morning meal.

FISH TO IMPRESS

SERVES 4

INGREDIENTS

4 tilapia fillets
1/3 cup (80 ml) butter
1/3 cup (80 ml) breadcrumbs
1-inch piece fresh ginger, peeled and grated
Juice of 1 lime
3 tbsp soy sauce
1 tsp hot sauce (or to taste)
1/4 cup (60 ml) fresh cilantro, chopped

PREPARATION

Let butter soften in a bowl for 15 minutes. With a fork, mash together all ingredients, except fish, until mixture becomes a paste.

Pour a bit of oil onto a baking sheet. Place fish on the baking sheet and spread breadcrumb mixture over tilapia to form a crust.

Cook in a 400°F (200°C) oven for 15 minutes, or until fish flakes easily with a fork.

This is the ultimate dish to impress your parents with your newfound culinary skills!

QUICK RISOTTO

SERVES 2

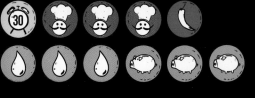

CHEF'S TIP

Before taking your risotto off the heat, taste the rice to see if it's cooked. If it's still not completely cooked, add a bit of water and continue cooking until *al dente*, which means that it should be slightly firm to the bite, but not crunchy.

GOURMET VARIATION

Now that you've mastered the art of making a simple risotto, try it with different vegetables, meat, or seafood; use beef or veal stock instead of chicken stock; or substitute the Parmesan with another one of your favorite cheeses!

INGREDIENTS

1 tbsp olive oil or vegetable oil
1 onion, chopped
6 slices pancetta, salami, or ham, cut into thin strips
8 button mushrooms, quartered
1/2 cup (125 ml) Arborio rice (also known as Italian rice)
2 cups (500 ml) chicken stock
1 cup (250 ml) baby spinach
1/4 cup (60 ml) fresh Parmesan cheese, grated
1 tbsp butter
Salt and pepper

PREPARATION

In a large pot, heat oil.

Add onion and cook for 2 minutes.

Add meat and mushrooms and cook for another 2 minutes.

Add rice and cook, stirring, for 30 seconds.

Add chicken stock. Let simmer gently for 15 minutes, stirring every 3 minutes.

Add baby spinach and mix well to make sure it cooks.

Finish by adding Parmesan cheese and butter. Stir continuously for 1 minute. Season with salt and pepper and serve.

BEANS TO THE RESCUE!

SERVES 2

INGREDIENTS

1 can (19 oz) mixed beans, drained and rinsed
1 can (7 oz) whole kernel corn, drained and rinsed
1 cucumber, halved lengthwise and sliced into half-moons
Salt and pepper

FOR VINAIGRETTE

1/4 cup (60 ml) olive oil
2 tbsp balsamic vinegar
1 tbsp honey
A few drops hot sauce
1 tbsp Italian seasoning

PREPARATION

Combine vinaigrette ingredients. Add beans, corn, and cucumber and season with salt and pepper. Mix well and serve.

CRÊPES

SERVES 2

INGREDIENTS

2 eggs
1 cup (250 ml) milk
1 tbsp sugar
1 pinch salt
A few drops vanilla extract (optional)
3/4 cup (180 ml) flour
1 tbsp butter

PREPARATION

Whisk together eggs, milk, sugar, salt, and vanilla extract. Gradually sprinkle in flour, whisking constantly to prevent lumps from forming. In a non-stick pan, cook 6 large crêpes, one at a time, over medium heat. Use a bit of butter to cook each pancake. Serve.

GOURMET VARIATION

For high-fiber pancakes, replace half of the white flour with 1/2 cup (125 ml) buckwheat flour.

CHEF'S TIP

Use a paper towel to grease the pan with just a little bit of butter. You won't use as much and your crêpes will turn out perfectly golden!

26

TROPICAL VACATION CHICKEN

SERVES 4

 CHEF'S TIP

Zest is made from peeling or scraping the flavorful, fragrant outer skin of citrus fruits. To add a bit of zest to your recipe, simply grate the peel of the lime before juicing, avoiding the bitter white layer (pith) under the peel.

 GOURMET VARIATION

If you love seafood, try this dish with shrimp instead of chicken!

INGREDIENTS

---

1 tbsp olive oil or vegetable oil
2 boneless skinless chicken breasts,
cut into 1- to 1-1/2-inch cubes
1/2 red onion, thinly sliced
1 can (14 oz) sliced peaches, drained and rinsed
1 can (6 oz) coconut milk
1 cup water or chicken stock
Juice of 1 lime
Salt and pepper
1 cup (250 ml) couscous

PREPARATION

In a large pan, heat oil and sauté chicken and onion for 2 minutes. Add peaches, coconut milk, water or stock, and lime juice. Season with salt and pepper and let simmer for 5 minutes. Add couscous and stir. Remove from heat, cover, and let sit for 5 minutes. Serve.

VEGGIE STIR-FRY

SERVES 2

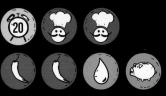

GOURMET VARIATION

Not sure what to do with that meat, seafood, or tofu sitting in the fridge? Slice it into strips and toss it in your stir-fry along with the vegetables.

DID YOU KNOW?

In Asia, rice noodles are used in many dishes, including desserts like *kheer*, a rice pudding made by boiling rice vermicelli with milk and sugar, and then adding cardamom, saffron, raisins, and nuts.

INGREDIENTS

---

2 squares (about 4 oz) rice noodles
2 tbsp vegetable oil
1 onion, thinly sliced
2 cups (500 ml) vegetables of your choice, thinly sliced (carrots, peppers, broccoli, zucchini, mushrooms, green beans, corn, etc.)
1/4 cup (60 ml) soy sauce
A few drops hot sauce (optional)
2 eggs

PREPARATION

Bring a small pot of water to a boil. Soak noodles for 5 minutes. Stir gently with a fork to separate noodles and then drain.

In a pan, heat vegetable oil and cook onion and vegetables until soft. Add soy sauce, hot sauce, and noodles. Mix well.

Break eggs into pan and stir quickly to incorporate. Let cook, undisturbed, for 30 seconds. Mix well and serve.

28

FISH BURGER

SERVES 1

INGREDIENTS

1/2 fillet (about 1/4 lb) white fish (haddock, halibut, plaice, etc.)
Salt and pepper
1 tbsp flour
1 egg
2 tbsp breadcrumbs
2 tbsp olive oil or vegetable oil
1 bun of your choice
Mayonnaise (to taste)
A few slices tomato

PREPARATION

Place fish fillet on a large plate and season with salt and pepper.

Coat fish in a thin layer of flour.

Break egg into a bowl and beat with a fork.

Dip fish in egg. Coat thoroughly.

Coat fish with breadcrumb mixture and press in firmly with your hands to make sure breadcrumb mixture sticks to fish.

Heat oil in a large pan over medium heat and sear fish on each side for 2 to 3 minutes until both sides are golden brown.

Top bun with mayonnaise, tomato slices, and fish. Add other toppings if desired (pickled hot peppers, lettuce, cheese, pickles, etc.).

 **DID YOU KNOW?**

The culinary method in this recipe is called "breading," which is the process of coating food (usually meat, vegetables, fish, seafood, or tofu) with breadcrumbs, flour, or cornmeal mixed with seasoning. Breading is well-suited to frying, because it creates a deliciously crispy golden crust.

29

TROUT "EN PAPILLOTE"

SERVES 2

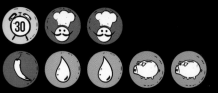

INGREDIENTS

12 asparagus spears
2 trout fillets (about 1/2 lb each)
Salt and pepper
2 cloves garlic, thinly sliced
1 lemon, sliced
2 tbsp olive oil

PREPARATION

With your hands, snap off the tough bottom ends of the asparagus (they will break naturally where the spears become tender).

Tear off 2 sheets of aluminum foil (about 15 inches each).

Place asparagus on one sheet of aluminum foil and top with trout fillets. Season with salt and pepper. Sprinkle garlic over trout and asparagus and top with lemon slices. Drizzle olive oil over everything.

Cover with the second sheet of aluminum foil.

Fold over the edges of the aluminum foil and crimp to seal fish in tightly.

Cook in a 350°F (175°C) oven for 15 minutes.

Remove from oven, carefully open foil, and serve.

CHEF'S TIP

Asparagus and trout are a great combination *en papillote* (in a parcel) because they take the same amount of time to cook. If you're not a fan of asparagus, remember to choose another vegetable with an identical cooking time.

CHICKEN & BROCCOLI POT PIE

SERVES 4

INGREDIENTS

4 boneless skinless chicken thighs, cut into 1-inch cubes
1 broccoli, cut into small florets
1 can (10 oz) cream of broccoli soup
1 can (10 oz) cream of chicken soup
1 cup (250 ml) Gruyere cheese, grated
4 slices bread, cubed
2 tbsp olive oil or vegetable oil
1/2 tsp salt

PREPARATION

In a large bowl, combine all ingredients except bread, oil, and salt. Mix well and put into a large casserole dish. Cook in a 350°F (175°C) oven for 30 minutes.

In a bowl, toss cubed bread with oil and salt. Remove casserole from oven, spread bread evenly over the top, and put back in the oven. Cook for another 15 minutes or until croutons are golden brown.

GRILLED MUSHROOMS

SERVES 2

INGREDIENTS

1 tbsp butter
10 button mushrooms, halved
or 2 portobello mushrooms, cut into 1/4-inch slices
2 cloves garlic, chopped
1 tsp steak spice
1 tbsp balsamic vinegar

PREPARATION

In a pan: In a large pan, heat butter over high heat, being careful not to let it burn. Add mushrooms and let cook, undisturbed, for 1 minute to let them brown. Stir and cook for another minute. Add garlic, steak spice, and vinegar. Stir again and cook for a few seconds longer. Serve.

On the barbecue: If you're barbecuing, use portobello mushrooms. Instead of butter, use 2 tbsp vegetable oil and combine all ingredients in a bowl, including oil. Grill mushrooms for 30 seconds on each side. Absolutely delicious!

DID YOU KNOW?

Portobellos are perfect for new vegetarians or just for people who want to eat more vegetables—the mushrooms have a chewy, meaty texture and a rich, earthy flavor.

CORN CHOWDER

SERVES 4

INGREDIENTS

1 tbsp olive oil or vegetable oil
4 slices bacon, cut into small pieces
2 carrots, peeled and grated
1 can (14 oz) creamed corn
1 can (10 oz) cream of chicken soup
1/2 cup (125 ml) water
Salt and pepper

PREPARATION

In a large pot, heat oil and cook bacon. Add carrots and creamed corn. Cook for 1 minute and then add remaining ingredients. Mix well and let simmer gently for 15 minutes. Serve.

 **DID YOU KNOW?**

If you can't find creamed corn, use a can of whole kernel corn instead.

BURGERS WITH CARAMELIZED ONIONS

SERVES 6

FOR BURGERS

2 lbs ground beef
1/3 cup (80 ml) ketchup
3 tbsp steak spice
1 large onion, finely chopped

6 hamburger buns

6 slices cheese of your choice

FOR CARAMELIZED ONIONS

4 white onions, thinly sliced
1 tbsp butter
2 tbsp sugar
1/2 cup (125 ml) water
Salt and pepper

PREPARATION

In a pot, melt butter over medium heat and cook onions and sugar for 15 minutes, stirring often. When the bottom of the pot begins to brown, add water and continue cooking until liquid has evaporated. Season with salt and pepper.

Combine burger ingredients and form 6 medium-sized patties.

Cook patties in a pan or on the barbecue for 5 to 7 minutes on each side. Top with cheese slices 2 minutes before removing from heat.

Toast buns. Top with patties, caramelized onions, and your favorite toppings.

34

PITA PIZZAS

SERVES 4

FOR TOMATO SAUCE

1 can (28 oz) whole tomatoes
1 tsp sugar
2 tbsp olive oil
1 tbsp Italian seasoning
1/2 tsp salt
2 cloves garlic, chopped

FOR PIZZA

4 pitas
1 cup (250 ml) grated cheese of your choice
Meat of your choice
(ham, salami, pepperoni, prosciutto, bacon, anchovies, etc.)
Marinated vegetables of your choice, thinly sliced
(sundried tomatoes, hearts of palm, eggplant, artichokes, olives, etc.)
Fresh vegetables of your choice, thinly sliced
(mushrooms, peppers, onions, tomatoes, zucchini, spinach, etc.)

PREPARATION

Pour tomatoes into a colander, crush slightly, and let liquid drain. In a bowl, combine tomatoes and remaining sauce ingredients. Mix with your hands to keep sauce chunky.

Spread sauce over pitas and top with meat, vegetables, and cheese. Cook in a 400°F (200°C) oven for 15 minutes.

GOURMET VARIATION

If you've got naan, tortillas, baguette, or any other bread at home that you don't want to waste, use it instead of pitas!

SUPERSAVER'S TIP

Have a pizza party—you provide the pitas, sauce, and cheese, and let your guests bring their favorite toppings!

MEATBALLS & MUSHROOMS

SERVES 4

FOR MEATBALLS

1 lb ground beef
1 tbsp steak spice
1 egg
1/4 cup (60 ml) breadcrumbs
Salt and pepper

FOR SAUCE

1 tbsp vegetable oil
2 cups (500 ml) button mushrooms, quartered
2 cups (500 ml) water
1 tsp Dijon mustard
1 packet (1 oz) store-bought demi-glace

PREPARATION

Combine meatball ingredients. Form into 1-inch balls and refrigerate.

In a large pot, heat oil and sauté mushrooms. Add water, mustard, and demi-glace and mix well to prevent lumps from forming. Bring to a boil and add meatballs. Cover and cook for 15 minutes over low heat.

Serve over rice, mashed potatoes, pasta, or couscous.

GOURMET VARIATION

Don't feel bad about not eating your vegetables—this comforting meal tastes even better with broccoli, turnips or carrots added to the sauce.

36

PORK, APPLES & CHEDDAR

SERVES 2

INGREDIENTS

1 tbsp honey
2 tbsp butter
1 apple, cored and thinly sliced
2 boneless pork chops (about 1/2-inch thick)
Salt and pepper
2 slices cheddar or Emmental (Swiss) cheese

PREPARATION

In a pan, melt honey and 1 tbsp butter and cook apples for 2 minutes, or until soft. Transfer to a bowl and set aside.

In the same pan, melt remaining butter and cook pork chops for 2 minutes. Season with salt and pepper. Flip and top with apples and cheese. Cook for another 3 minutes and serve.

GOURMET VARIATION

For a beautiful presentation, why not serve your pork chops on a bed of arugula or mixed greens?

37

DRESSED-UP GREEN BEANS

SERVES 2

INGREDIENTS

4 cups green beans
2 tbsp butter
2 cloves garlic, minced
1/4 cup (60 ml) black olives, rinsed, pitted, and sliced into rounds
1/4 cup (60 ml) fresh parsley, chopped
1/4 cup (60 ml) feta cheese, crumbled
Salt and pepper

PREPARATION

Bring a large pot of salted water to a boil.

Cut tops (stems) off green beans.

Put green beans into boiling water and cook for 1 minute. Drain. Return pot to stove and melt butter. Add garlic and olives and stir. Add green beans, feta, and parsley. Season with salt and pepper, mix well, and serve.

GERMAN SAUERKRAUT

SERVES 4

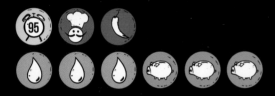

INGREDIENTS

12 new potatoes
4 sausages of your choice, cut in half
1 lb cooked or smoked ham, thickly sliced
1 jar (32 oz) sauerkraut, drained
1 bottle (12 oz) dark beer

Dijon mustard and sour cream on the side

PREPARATION

Place potatoes, sausages and ham in an oven-safe casserole dish. Cover with sauerkraut and beer. Cover and cook in a 350°F (175°C) oven for 1 hour 30 minutes. Serve with Dijon mustard and sour cream.

Sauerkraut dishes are traditionally seasoned with bay leaves and juniper berries. If you have these spices on hand, add them right before putting the casserole into the oven.

 GOURMET VARIATION

Apples and sauerkraut are a winning combination—just grate a couple of apples and stir into the sauerkraut before cooking. It's very important to drain and thoroughly rinse the sauerkraut before cooking to remove the sour taste of the wine marinade.

 CHEF'S TIP

This is the perfect one-dish meal to serve at casual dinner parties. Place the dish in the middle of the table so everyone can help themselves!

39

BREAKFAST FOR TWO

SERVES 2

GOURMET VARIATION

Set out a condiment tray with sides of mayonnaise, ketchup, salsa, real maple syrup, tomatoes, spinach, etc., for a build-your-own breakfast!

INGREDIENTS

4 eggs
Salt and pepper
1 tbsp butter
4 slices ham, diced
2 tbsp goat cheese, crumbled

2 English muffins

PREPARATION

Break eggs into a small bowl and whisk with a fork. Season with salt and pepper.

In a pan, heat butter and sauté ham. Add eggs and goat cheese. Stir until eggs are cooked and serve on toasted English muffins.

CHEESE & TOMATO TART

SERVES 4

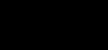

INGREDIENTS

1 sheet store-bought puff pastry, thawed
2 tbsp Dijon mustard
6 slices Swiss cheese
4 tomatoes, sliced
Salt and pepper
2 tbsp olive oil
1 tbsp Italian seasoning

PREPARATION

Sprinkle a bit of flour onto a rolling pin (or an empty or full wine or beer bottle). Roll out puff pastry into a thin rectangle, about 12 inches x 8 inches, and place on an oiled baking sheet.

Brush Dijon mustard over the entire surface of the puff pastry. Arrange cheese slices on top and place tomato slices over cheese. Season with salt and pepper.

In a small bowl, combine olive oil and Italian seasoning and pour over tart. Cook in a 350°F (175°C) oven for 30 minutes. Serve.

 CHEF'S TIP

f you don't have a rolling pin, a full or empty wine or beer bottle will do the job just as well!

 DID YOU KNOW?

Puff pastry is actually many layers of very thin dough and fat, which, when combined, cause the dough to rise during baking. Unlike traditional pie pastry, puff pastry scraps can't be gathered together and rolled out again because the layers will puff up unevenly. For the best results, use the entire square of dough as is, or cut pieces as needed.

41

TORTELLINI ALLA GIGI

SERVES 2

INGREDIENTS

2 cups (500 ml) tortellini of your choice
1 tbsp olive oil or vegetable oil
8 button mushrooms, sliced
4 slices ham, cut into thin strips
1 cup (250 ml) tomato sauce, store-bought or homemade
1/2 cup (125 ml) 35% cream
Salt and pepper

PREPARATION

Cook tortellini in boiling water according to package directions. Drain and set aside.

In the same pot, heat oil. Add mushrooms and ham and cook for 2 minutes. Add tomato sauce, cream, and cooked tortellini, and let simmer for 2 minutes. Season with salt and pepper and serve.

BACK-TO-SCHOOL STEW

SERVES 4

INGREDIENTS

1 tbsp olive oil or vegetable oil
2 Italian sausages, hot or mild, cut into 1-inch rounds
2 onions, chopped
2 carrots, peeled and cut into rounds
8 new potatoes, halved
1 can (14 oz) diced tomatoes
1 cup (250 ml) beef stock
1 can (19 oz) brown lentils, drained and rinsed
1 tbsp Italian seasoning
Salt and pepper

PREPARATION

In a large pot, heat oil and add sausages, onions, carrots, and potatoes. Cook for 5 minutes without stirring. After 5 minutes, stir and cook for another 2 minutes. Add remaining ingredients and let simmer for 20 minutes, stirring occasionally. Serve with fresh bread.

SCHNITZEL

SERVES 2

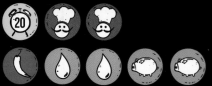

INGREDIENTS

2 boneless pork chops (about 1/2-inch thick)
Salt and pepper
2 tbsp Dijon mustard
1/4 cup (60 ml) Italian breadcrumbs
1 clove garlic, minced
2 tbsp fresh parsley, chopped
1/4 cup (60 ml) vegetable oil
1 lemon, cut into 4 wedges

PREPARATION

Place pork chops between two sheets of plastic wrap and flatten using a pot, a jar, a can, or a bottle. Season with salt and pepper and brush with Dijon mustard.

Combine breadcrumbs, garlic, and parsley. Coat pork chops with breadcrumb mixture and press in firmly with your hands to make sure coating sticks to pork chops.

In a large pan, heat oil and carefully place pork chops in pan. When coating starts to turn golden brown on the bottom, flip and cook until the other side turns golden brown. Remove from heat and serve with lemon wedges.

GOURMET VARIATION

Schnitzel works just as well with chicken. Just slice a chicken breast into two thin cutlets and follow the recipe!

DID YOU KNOW?

This traditional Austrian dish is usually served with potato salad or potatoes with butter and parsley.

LEEK & POTATO SOUP

SERVES 4

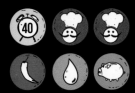

INGREDIENTS

1 tbsp butter
1 onion, thinly sliced
2 cloves garlic, quartered
1 leek, thinly sliced (remove and discard 1/4 of green tops)
2 yellow-fleshed potatoes, peeled and cut into large cubes
4 cups chicken or vegetable stock
1 tsp salt
Pepper

PREPARATION

In a colander, carefully rinse sliced leek to remove any dirt.

In a large pot, melt butter and cook onion, garlic and leek for 5 minutes or until soft. Add potatoes and stock. Season with salt and pepper and let simmer for 20 minutes.

Purée with a hand blender.

GOURMET VARIATION

Turn your soup into a gratin! Ladle some soup into an oven-safe bowl and top with a slice of toast and a generous layer of your favorite cheese. Broil in the oven for 1 to 2 minutes.

DID YOU KNOW?

Yellow-fleshed potatoes, like the Yukon Gold variety, have yellow-tinged, waxy, moist flesh and a sweet flavor that make them perfect for boiling, baking and frying.

BAKED POTATO SKINS

SERVES 4

INGREDIENTS

6 Russet potatoes (small or medium)
2 tbsp vegetable oil
Salt and pepper
6 slices bacon, diced
2 tbsp store-bought barbecue sauce
1 cup (250 ml) old cheddar cheese, grated

Sour cream
Fresh chives, chopped (optional)

PREPARATION

Wash potatoes thoroughly and cut in half lengthwise.

In a bowl, toss potatoes in vegetable oil and season with salt and pepper. Place potatoes, cut side down, on a baking sheet covered in parchment paper and cook in a 400°F (200°C) oven for 30 minutes. Let cool.

With a spoon, scoop out potato flesh, leaving about 1/4 of the flesh in the skins. Save scooped out flesh.

In a pan, cook bacon. Add barbecue sauce right before removing from heat. Divide bacon equally between potato skins, sprinkle with cheese, and broil in the oven for 3 to 5 minutes. Serve with sour cream and a few chives.

GOURMET VARIATION

Stuff your potato skins with any number of your favorite toppings. Try shredded chicken, ground beef, blue cheese or salsa, or go vegetarian by adding tofu or veggie bacon.

CHEF'S TIP

The best way to use up the extra potato flesh is to make mashed potatoes! (See recipe on page 038.)

MAC & CHEESE

SERVES 2

INGREDIENTS

2 cups (500 ml) macaroni
1 tbsp butter
1 tbsp flour
1 tsp Dijon mustard
2 cups (500 ml) milk
1 cup (250 ml) old cheddar or Gruyere cheese, grated
Salt and pepper

PREPARATION

Cook pasta in a large pot of boiling water according to package directions. Drain.

In a pot, melt butter, add flour, and whisk for 10 seconds. Add mustard and 1/4 cup (125 ml) milk. Whisk until smooth. Slowly pour in remaining milk while continuing to whisk to completely dissolve flour and prevent lumps from forming. Bring sauce to a gentle boil, stirring constantly. When sauce starts to bubble, add cheese and stir until melted. Add macaroni, mix well, and serve.

WINNING CHICKEN WINGS

24 CHICKEN WINGS

GOURMET VARIATION

Kick it up a notch by serving dipping sauces like ranch, blue cheese, or honey mustard on the side!

INGREDIENTS

24 chicken wings
1/4 cup (60 ml) ketchup
2 tbsp white vinegar
2 tbsp sugar
2 tbsp hot sauce
1 tbsp steak spice

PREPARATION

In a large bowl, combine all ingredients. Let marinate in the refrigerator for at least 2 hours. Place chicken wings on an oiled baking sheet and cook in a 400°F (200°C) oven for 30 minutes. Flip wings and cook for another 30 minutes. Serve.

THE FRITTATA

SERVES 4

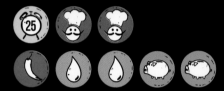

INGREDIENTS

6 eggs
1/2 cup (125 ml) milk
1 cup (250 ml) Gruyere cheese, grated
Salt and pepper

1 tbsp olive oil or vegetable oil
1 broccoli, cut into small florets
5 slices bacon, cut into small strips

PREPARATION

In a bowl, whisk together eggs, milk, and cheese.

In a non-stick pan, heat oil and cook bacon and broccoli for 3 to 5 minutes. Pour egg mixture into pan, cover with a lid, a large plate, or aluminum foil, and cook over low heat for 15 minutes. Serve.

 CHEF'S TIP

To serve your frittata, cover the pan with a plate that is bigger than the pan and flip!

GREEK SALAD

SERVES 4

INGREDIENTS

1/2 cup (125 ml) feta cheese, crumbled
12 cherry tomatoes, halved
1 cucumber, cut into cubes
1/2 red onion, thinly sliced
1/4 cup (60 ml) olive oil
2 tbsp white wine vinegar, red wine vinegar, or balsamic vinegar
Salt and pepper

PREPARATION

Combine all ingredients. Mix and enjoy.

 **CHEF'S TIP**

Greek salad can be prepared in advance and will keep for several days in the fridge.

 GOURMET VARIATION

Add a handful of Kalamata olives, or a pinch of oregano, if you have some on hand. And for a complete meal, throw in some grilled chicken!

50

CHILI SIN CARNE

SERVES 6

FOR CHILI

1 tbsp olive oil or vegetable oil
1 onion, finely chopped
2 cloves garlic, minced
2 red peppers, diced
1 tbsp cumin
1 tbsp chili powder
1 can (19 oz) red kidney beans, drained and rinsed
1 can (28 oz) diced tomatoes
1 can (11 oz) whole kernel corn, drained and rinsed
Salt and pepper
1 cup (250 ml) green beans, chopped
1/4 cup (60 ml) fresh cilantro, chopped (optional)

PREPARATION

In a pot, heat oil and sauté onion, garlic, and red peppers for 5 minutes. Stir in cumin and chili powder. Add red kidney beans, tomatoes, and corn. Season with salt and pepper and let simmer for 15 minutes. Add green beans and cilantro and cook for another 2 minutes. Remove from heat.

Top with sour cream and grated cheese.

Serve with fresh bread or corn chips on the side.

DID YOU KNOW?

Chili con carne (chili with meat) has been the official dish of Texas since 1977.

51

RED PEPPER HUMMUS

SERVES 4

INGREDIENTS

1 red pepper, seeded and cut into strips
2 cloves garlic, halved
1 can (19 oz) chickpeas, drained and rinsed
2 tbsp tahini
1/3 cup (80 ml) olive oil
Juice of 1 lemon
Salt and pepper

PREPARATION

In a pan, heat 1 tbsp olive oil and sauté pepper and garlic for 2 to 3 minutes.

In a large bowl, combine all ingredients and purée with a hand blender. Season with salt and pepper.

Serve with fresh pita bread, chips, veggies, or as a sandwich spread.

 GOURMET VARIATION

The best thing about hummus is that you can add almost anything to it! Try roasted eggplant, hot peppers, sundried tomatoes, onions, olives, and even pumpkin. As long as you've got tahini, you're all set.

52

SWEET & SOUR DRUMSTICKS

SERVES 6

INGREDIENTS

6 chicken drumsticks with skin
1/4 cup (60 ml) honey
1/4 cup (60 ml) soy sauce
1 tsp chili powder
1 tbsp olive oil or vegetable oil

PREPARATION

In a bowl, combine honey, soy sauce, and chili powder.

In a pan, heat oil and sear chicken.

Pour sauce into pan. Cover and cook for 10 minutes. Remove cover and cook over medium heat for 5 to 8 minutes longer, or until sauce is thick and coats drumsticks. Serve.

CLASSIC COLESLAW

SERVES 4

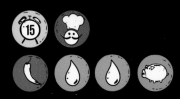

INGREDIENTS

1/2 green cabbage, grated or very thinly sliced (about 4 cups)
1 carrot, grated
1/2 onion, grated

FOR VINAIGRETTE

1/4 cup (60 ml) white vinegar
1 tbsp sugar
1/2 cup (125 ml) vegetable oil
1 tsp Dijon mustard
1 pinch Italian seasoning
Salt and pepper

PREPARATION

In a large bowl, combine vinaigrette ingredients. Add vegetables. Season with salt and pepper and mix well. For maximum flavor, refrigerate for about 2 hours before serving.

 **GOURMET VARIATION**

Pair this salad with saucy chicken drumsticks (see recipe on page 154), roast chicken (see recipe on page 170), or chicken wings (see recipe on page 142).

54

SAVORY DILL & FETA "DOUGHNUTS"

SERVES 2

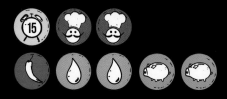

INGREDIENTS

2 zucchinis
1/2 cup (125 ml) feta cheese, crumbled
1/4 cup (60 ml) flour
1/2 tsp baking powder
1/4 cup (60 ml) fresh dill, chopped
Salt and pepper
2 tbsp olive oil or vegetable oil

PREPARATION

Grate zucchinis into a bowl. Add feta cheese, flour, baking powder, and dill. Season with salt and pepper and mix well with a spoon to make a dough.

In a non-stick pan, heat oil and cook a few spoonfuls of dough at a time. When doughnut bottoms begin to turn golden brown, flip and continue to cook until golden brown. Serve with plain yogurt, tzatziki, or any other sauce of your choice.

 DID YOU KNOW?

Fresh and dried dill is a favorite ingredient across Scandinavia and Eastern Europe. It's delicious when married with dairy, and is one of the most popular pickling herbs.

APPLE CRISP

SERVES 4

INGREDIENTS

1 tbsp butter
4 apples, cored and sliced
2 tbsp brown sugar
1/2 tsp cinnamon

FOR TOPPING

1/2 cup (125 ml) flour
1-1/2 cups (375 ml) oats
1/2 cup (125 ml) brown sugar
1/2 cup (125 ml) butter, melted
Salt

PREPARATION

Grease an 8-inch x 8-inch baking dish with butter.

In a bowl, combine apples, brown sugar, and cinnamon. Spread apples evenly at the bottom of the baking dish.

In the same bowl, combine all topping ingredients. Distribute topping evenly over apples. Bake in a 350°F (175°C) oven for 40 minutes or until topping is golden brown.

GOURMET VARIATION

Why limit yourself to apple crisp? Try a different fruit every time: mixed berries, pears, stone fruits like peaches and plums, or even sweet-and-sour rhubarb.

56

THE CROQUE-MONSIEUR

SERVES 2

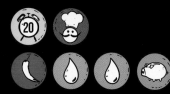

 **GOURMET VARIATION**

There's more than one way to make a croque-monsieur! This classic French sandwich can be made with almost any meat, cheese, or veggies you've got in your fridge. It's fast, inexpensive, and the perfect student meal.

Here are a few combinations to get you started:

- Swiss cheese, ham, and apple slices
- Tomato sauce, pepperoni, and mozzarella
- Brie, spinach, olives, and sundried tomatoes
- Cream cheese, smoked salmon, and thinly sliced red onion
- Goat cheese, ham, and mushrooms

INGREDIENTS

2 slices bread of your choice
2 slices Swiss cheese
2 slices ham or lunchmeat of your choice
4 leaves fresh basil (optional)
4 slices tomato
Salt and pepper
2 tbsp fresh Parmesan cheese, grated (optional)

PREPARATION

Place bread on a baking sheet. Top with cheese, lunchmeat, basil, and tomato slices. Season with salt and pepper and sprinkle with Parmesan cheese.

Place baking sheet on bottom oven rack and cook at 350°F (175°C) for 10 minutes, then raise oven temperature to broil and continue cooking for 3 minutes. Serve hot.

57

CELERIAC SALAD

SERVES 4

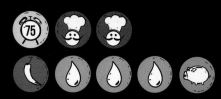

INGREDIENTS

1 small celeriac
2 tbsp mayonnaise
1 tbsp Dijon mustard
Juice of 1/2 lemon
Salt and pepper
1/4 cup (60 ml) fresh tarragon (optional)
2 tbsp water

PREPARATION

Cut off both ends of celeriac to create a flat surface that will keep it steady on the cutting board.

Peel celeriac with a knife.

Grate peeled celeriac. To make it easier, cut into 4 pieces.

In a large bowl, combine all ingredients and refrigerate for at least 1 hour before serving.

 CHEF'S TIP

Like coleslaw, the longer this salad marinates, the better it tastes. It keeps in the refrigerator for several days.

GOURMET VARIATION

Add grated green apple for a fruity twist!

QUESADILLAS

SERVES 4

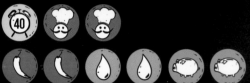

FOR BEANS

1/2 can (about 9-1/2 oz) black beans, drained and rinsed
1/4 cup (60 ml) olive oil
Hot sauce to taste
Salt and pepper

FOR VEGETABLES

1 tbsp olive oil
1 red pepper, cut into thin strips
1 onion, thinly sliced
1 tsp cumin

8 corn tortillas
4 slices Monterey jack cheese

PREPARATION

With a hand blender, purée black beans and olive oil. Add hot sauce to taste and season with salt and pepper.

In a pan, heat 1 tbsp olive oil and sauté onion and pepper until soft. Stir in cumin. Set aside.

Spread black bean mixture over 4 tortillas and top with veggies, Monterey jack cheese, and remaining 4 tortillas.

Brush top tortillas with a bit of olive oil and place on a baking sheet and cook in a 350°F (175°C) oven for 25 minutes.

Cut quesadillas into 4 slices and serve plain or with sour cream, salsa, or guacamole.

 **CHEF'S TIP**

If you don't have a hand blender, just use your hands to mash the beans!

59

BBQ CHICKEN

SERVES 4

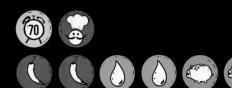

INGREDIENTS

1 whole chicken
2 tbsp olive oil
3 tbsp store-bought barbecue seasoning
2 onions, peeled and halved

PREPARATION

In a small bowl, combine olive oil and barbecue seasoning. Rub entire chicken with mixture.

Put onions inside chicken and place in an oven-safe casserole dish. Cook in a 350°F (175°C) oven for 1 hour. Halfway through cooking, remove chicken from oven, baste with the liquid at the bottom of the dish, and put back in oven.

When chicken is fully cooked through, remove from oven, carve, and serve.

60

FRENCH TOAST

SERVES 2

INGREDIENTS

4 slices bread of your choice
(baguette, brioche, raisin bread, etc.)
2 eggs
2 tbsp sugar
1/2 cup (125 ml) milk
1/2 tsp cinnamon

2 tbsp butter

PREPARATION

Break eggs into a large bowl. Add sugar, milk, and cinnamon, and whisk together with a fork.

Heat a pan over medium heat. Dip bread in egg mixture, making sure each slice is completely coated. Heat 1/2 tbsp butter, place one slice in the pan, and cook until bottom is golden brown. Flip and cook until the other side is golden brown. Repeat with remaining slices.

Serve with chocolate sauce (see recipe on page 036) or dulce de leche (see recipe on page 040).

INGREDIENTS INDEX

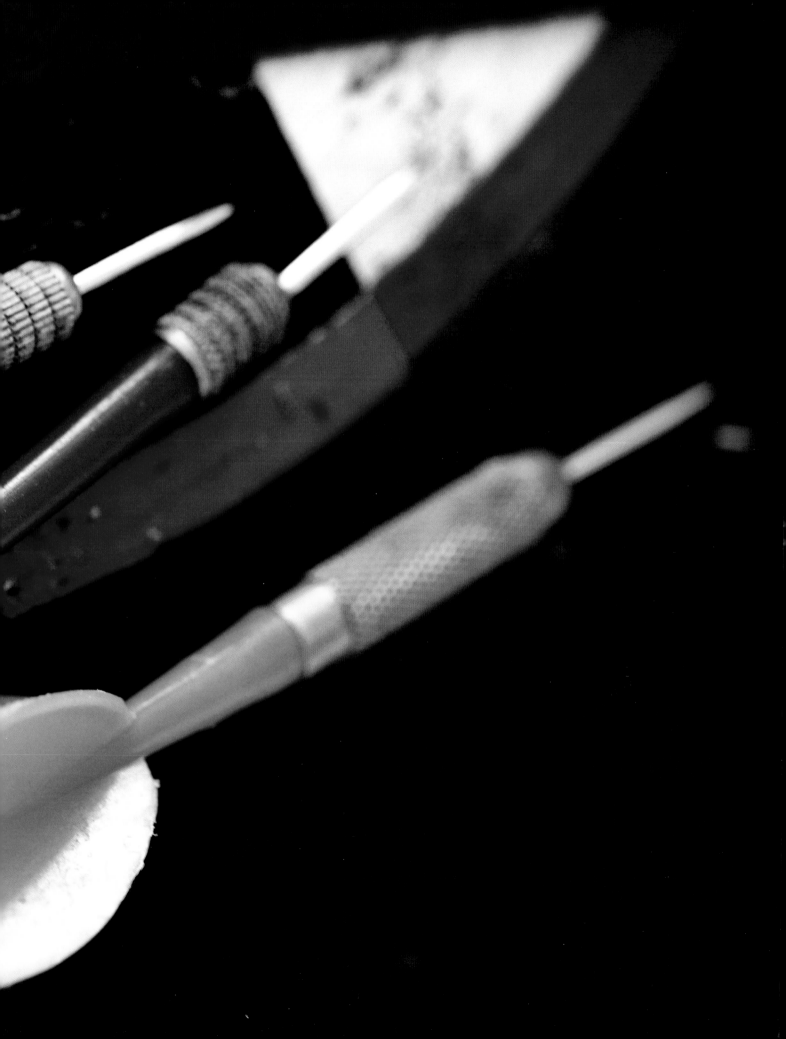

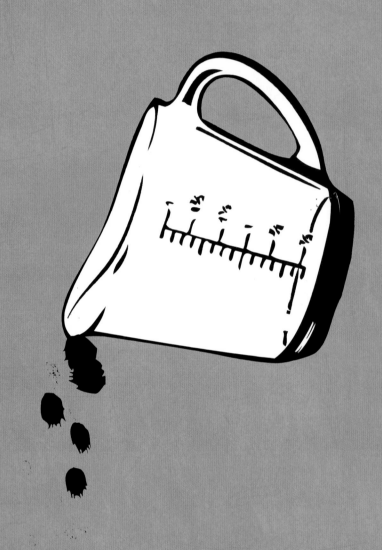

CONVERSION CHART

1 dl	10 cl	100 ml
1 tablespoon		15 ml
1 teaspoon		5 ml
1 oz.		30 ml
1 cup		250 ml
4 cups		1 l
1/2 cup		125 ml
1/4 cup		60 ml
1/3 cup		80 ml
1 lb		450 g
2 lbs		900 g
2.2 lbs		1 kg
400°F	200°C	T/7
350°F	175°C	T/6
300°F	150°C	T/5

Volume Conversion
* Approximate values

---

1 cup (250 ml) crumbled cheese	150 g
1 cup (250 ml) all-purpose flour	115 g
1 cup (250 ml) white sugar	200 g
1 cup (250 ml) brown sugar	220 g
1 cup (250 ml) butter	230 g
1 cup (250 ml) oil	215 g
1 cup (250 ml) canned tomatoes	250 g

NOTES

60

IN THE SAME COLLECTION

THE WORLD'S **60** BEST
SALADS
PERIOD.

THE WORLD'S **60** BEST
PASTA SAUCES
PERIOD.

THE WORLD'S **60** BEST
BURGERS
PERIOD.

THE WORLD'S **60** BEST
LUNCHES
PERIOD.

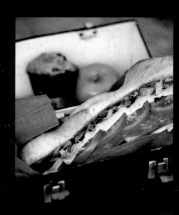